CELEBRATE
Great Quilts!
circa 1825–1940

Karey Patterson Bresenhan and Nancy O'Bryant Puentes

THE INTERNATIONAL QUILT FESTIVAL COLLECTION

C&T PUBLISHING

Text and Artwork © 2004 Karey Patterson Bresenhan
and Nancy O'Bryant Puentes
Publisher: Amy Marson
Editorial Director: Gailen Runge
Editor: Amy Marson
Technical Editor: Jan Grigsby
Proofreader: Stacy Chamness
Cover Designer: Kristy A. Konitzer
Design Director/Book Designer: Kristy A. Konitzer
Production Assistant: Tim Manibusan
Photography: Jim Lincoln, Jim Lincoln Photography
Published by C&T Publishing, Inc., P.O. Box 1456, Lafayette,
California, 94549
Front cover: Touching Stars
Back cover: Flowers & Birds Appliqué

Attention Teachers: C&T Publishing, Inc. encourages you to use this book as a
text for teaching. Contact us at 800-284-1114 or www.ctpub.com for more information about the C&T Teachers Program.

We take great care to ensure that the information included in this book is accurate
and presented in good faith, but no warranty is provided nor results guaranteed.
Having no control over the choices of materials or procedures used, neither the
authors nor C&T Publishing, Inc. shall have any liability to any person or entity
with respect to any loss or damage caused directly or indirectly by the information
contained in this book. For your convenience, we post an up-to-date listing of cor-
rections on our web page (www.ctpub.com). If a correction is not already noted,
please contact our customer service department at ctinfo@ctpub.com or at P.O. Box
1456, Lafayette, California, 94549.

Trademarked (™) and Registered Trademark (®) names are used throughout this
book. Rather than use the symbols with every occurrence of a trademark and registered trademark name, we are using the names only in the editorial fashion and to
the benefit of the owner, with no intention of infringement.

Library of Congress Cataloging-in-Publication Data

Bresenhan, Karey Patterson.
  Celebrate great quilts! circa 1820-1940 : the International Quilt Festival
collection / Karey Patterson Bresenhan & Nancy O'Bryant Puentes.
    p. cm.
  Includes bibliographical references and index.
  ISBN 1-57120-251-X (paper trade)
  1. Quilts--United States--Catalogs. 2. Quilts--Texas--Houston--Catalogs.
3. Quilts, Inc.--Catalogs. I. Puentes, Nancy O'Bryant. II. Title.
2. Karey Patterson Bresenhan

 NK9112.B6797 2004
 746.46'0973'074764235--dc22

2004001907

Printed in China
10 9 8 7 6 5 4 3 2 1

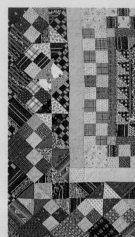

FROM THE TITLE PAGE:

Feathered Star with Compass Centers

Circa 1880; Missouri

*85" x 89" (21½" star block); Cotton; Hand
pieced, hand appliquéd, and hand quilted using
10–12 stitches per inch.*

An indigo and white Feathered Star with a
Compass or Sunburst center, this is hand pieced,
hand appliquéd, and hand quilted ten stitches to
the inch, sometimes twelve. A crisp design, this
quilt has a narrow inner indigo and white print
border, a wide muslin border, and an outer, wider
indigo and white border. Karey searched for six
years to find a "blue and white Feathered Star with
perfect quilting and something fancy in the center,"
before finding this gem.

CHARACTERISTICS OF QUILTS BY ERA

Examining the fabrics used in quilts is one of the best ways to distinguish the era in which a quilt was made, although there has always been incorporation of earlier fabrics into quilts. Care must be taken in dating quilts, therefore, and the following guide to fabrics used in quilts should be used only as a guide.

INTRODUCTION

Collect with your heart, not your head—that's the exact opposite of the best advice usually given to people assembling a collection, whether it is of arrowheads, art glass, or quilts. However, following our hearts over the past 30 years is the way we put together the quilt collection of the International Quilt Festival.

" We believe that a quilt must make your heart sing and your eyes dance. If it doesn't, then it's not meant for you."

It must appeal to your imagination as well as your sense of history and must all but mesmerize you. The right quilt should speak to you, make it impossible for you to forget it, and lure you back to see it over and over again. And every time you see it, you should see something new and special about it. If we had followed the standard wisdom in assembling Festival's collection, it would have a completely different look. Instead, our collection is personal and idiosyncratic, and the quilts delight us anew every time we see them.

In other words, we collect what we like. As cousins who are fifth-generation Texas quilters with the privilege of working within the quilt world as part of Festival, we like—indeed love—almost all quilts, so the Festival collection is wide-ranging, colorful, a little quirky, weighted toward fine workmanship, includes both classic design and folk art, and Star quilts of all kinds.

Often, we've stood before a quilt and puzzled over it. There would be something there that was atypical or a little odd. Sometimes the quilt would catch our attention even from a distance, and we'd know instinctively that there was something strange and wonderful about it. The person who owned the quilt at the time may not even have recognized this quality, but it spoke, loud and clear, to us.

Once a whitework quilt confounded us until we realized that its border was actually words, unreadable because the quilt had accidentally been hung upside-down. When it was righted, there was the signature ... not of the maker, but of the person who had marked the quilting design, the only quilt with this kind of attribution that we've ever seen. The lush coloration in a simple Nine-Patch Criss-Cross was strongly appealing, puzzling because the Nine-Patch is not one of our favorites. Then we discovered it was a Canadian Mennonite quilt, a genre entirely new to us. We remember the intricate quilting and the silky cotton sateen of the Horn of Plenty that triggered a déjà vu response, only to discover later that it was the last quilt to be sold from the same estate that had produced several others we had collected almost two decades earlier.

Another time, we found the charm of a folky Tree of Life—one single tree that dominated the whole quilt—amusing enough to collect even though it had only so-so handwork. The quilt brought a chuckle to everyone who saw it, and there's not enough laughter in life for us to have passed it up. Then there was the unusual Prairie

Flower—pieced, not appliquéd— that one of us, with a sinking heart and an empty bank account, once reluctantly sold, only to have it offered back to us many years later at the same price. We snatched it up, never to part with it again.

Every time we see the Contained Crazy Quilt made up of miniature blocks, found in Philadelphia and bought with the help of one of our mothers because it was too expensive to handle on our own, we see yet another delightful surprise in its tiny blocks. We're always amazed by the breathtaking chintz Rising Sun with its original glaze still intact that we collected from a Pennsylvania dealer who'd had a not-so-great

show and really, really wanted to make that sale. Then there's the Rose of Sharon variation, a super red and green appliqué that's showing its years with a mouse hole and a threadbare binding. Had we followed common collecting wisdom about choosing only quilts in pristine condition, that great quilt would still be languishing in Tennessee instead of charming viewers all over the country. And without dogged persistence, we'd never have found our superb indigo and white Feathered Star. It took six years, but finally someone in Missouri called us about the blue and white Feathered Star with lots of extraordinary quilting, tiny stitches, and something fancy—a Compass—in the center of each star.

Tree of Life variation, for quilt details see page 46

We've even collected quilts we didn't particularly like … but still, they spoke to our hearts. For example, we have a brown and gold Blazing Star found at a Quilt Day during the seven-year Texas Quilt Search that we conducted for the state's sesquicentennial in 1986. Neither one of us really likes this quilt—in fact, one of our husbands laughingly refers to it as a Valkyrie maiden's breastplate! We had a firm rule about never buying quilts or discussing dollar values at Quilt Days because we believed that this would create a conflict of interest. But at this Quilt Day, the person who brought the quilt stood up in the church where we were identifying the quilts

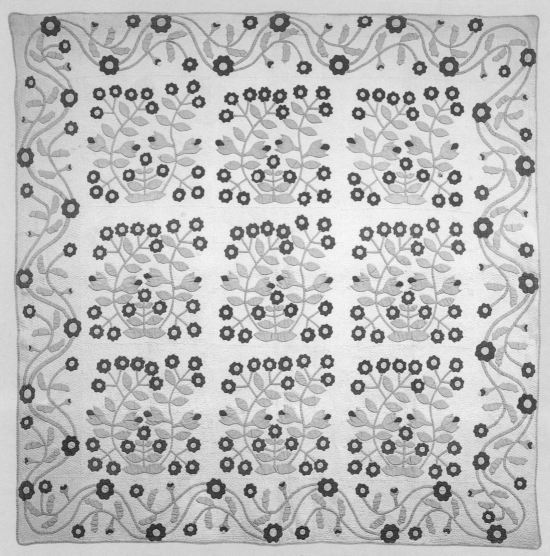

Oval Wreath with Flowers and Buds, for quilt details see page 18

and asked point blank: "How much is it worth?" When we told her that we never discussed the dollar value of the quilts, she became very upset and began telling us that we had to help, that the owner of the quilt was very sick, needed expensive medical treatment, and that this quilt was all she had left to sell. Our hearts ached for her. About to break our own long-standing rule, we caught sight of one of our mothers sidling toward the back of the church, where we knew, just knew, that she was going to buy the quilt from that lady the minute she left the church. We now have this quilt in our collection. Not a lovely quilt, perhaps, but what a lovely story it tells.

Rarely, we'll collect a quilt, then find another home for it several years later. Once we had a fine Lancaster County Amish wool quilt, a dramatic and very desirable Diamond in a Square. We lived with it, moved it around, put it on exhibit, tried to warm up to it, and finally decided that this quilt didn't speak to our hearts. We found another collector who was thrilled with it, and we knew we'd done the right thing. You have to be willing to keep a collection fresh and realize that your tastes can change.

Of course, there's the other side of that concept: sometimes the first piece you collect remains your very favorite. For us, this is a pale, elegant Southern quilt, the *Oval Wreath with Flowers and Buds*, that's quilted almost 20 stitches to the inch in places. In our opinion, the intricacy of the double vining border, the masterful workmanship, the invisible appliqué, and the lively design are only enhanced by the soft faded colors. Years ago, when one of us was still selling antique quilts, this quilt was added to her shop's inventory and hung on display to sell. Each time someone would look seriously at the quilt and move on, that young shop owner would surreptitiously raise the price so no one would buy it. Finally she realized it wasn't in her heart to sell that quilt, and it became the cornerstone of our collection.

"And oh, my stars, there are all those great Star quilts!"

We're enchanted by Star quilts, maybe because we're both from the Lone Star State. Maybe because our great-grandmother made a Star quilt for every Methodist minister who came to Sabinal, Texas. Maybe because we both received Star quilts for wedding presents, originally made by that same great-grandmother and later finished at a family quilting bee—a cherished memory for each of us. Whatever the reason, Star quilts not only speak to us, they cry out to us: "Me! Me! Look at me! Take me!"

We make no effort to ignore them, because we're star struck. We've collected a whole galaxy of them. For a Star quilt, we can even overlook mediocre quilting, and the collection reflects that passion. There are Touching Stars, Lone

Stars, Broken Stars, Stars of Bethlehem, String Pieced Stars, Feathered Stars, Blazing Stars, not one but two *Star Spangled Banner*, and that's not counting all the quilts with stars in and on them, like the *Ocean Wave with Stars* and *Flowers and Coxcombs with Stars*.

The other type of quilt that draws us like a magnet is the red and green appliqué, usually from the 1850s, 1860s, or 1870s. We like our appliqués to be either perfect or a bit eccentric. For example, our *Birds and Grapes Appliqué* combines the classic red and green Princess Feather design with a marvelous border featuring birds enjoying a feast of purple grapes. The quiltmaker's vision definitely exceeded her skills as can be seen in the irregularly shaped stars and flowers and in the off-center borders, yet the overall feel of the quilt is creative and celebratory. When compared to anoth-

Broken Star, for quilt details see page 57

er of our red and green quilts with similar design elements—the *Flowers and Birds* quilt—it's easy to see the dichotomy that characterizes our collection. Instead of being eccentric, this quilt is perfect, with its identical blocks and birds, its formal Swag and Bow border, and its elaborate trapunto. We acquired Bars and Roses, which was once part of the late Sandra Mitchell's collection, years after we first admired it, and it is as classic and mannered a red and green quilt as the *Birds and Grapes* is quirky.

Many people collect for rarity, age, or specific type of quilt; others collect as an investment, choosing those pieces that are sure to increase in value. Once again, this doesn't describe us. Trying to convince us to add a quilt to our collection because it is sure to escalate in value just doesn't do the trick, perhaps because we truly love these quilts and have no intention of parting with them! Very seldom do we collect for rarity or age alone. While we appreciate early eighteenth century quilts, they don't often come on the market at a level that fits our budget, and we generally prefer the brilliance of the dyes that became available after the mid-1850s. However, one of our treasures is from the first quarter of the nineteenth century: the *Calimanco Quilt*, c. 1820–30. These were usually wholecloth quilts and rarely embellished. However, this particular example seems to be a transition design, made by a master stitcher who was as much at home with the stylish embroidery more often seen earlier in the century as she was with the fine quilting typical of the period. The highly detailed floral embroidery closely resembles crewel work but is executed in much finer thread, a mark of embroidery expertise.

On the opposite end of the calendar, we also seek out remarkable twentieth century quilts, particularly those pastel beauties that are so much a trademark of the Depression Era, the 1930s. Often lightweight, with thin batting to allow fine stitching, these quilts are frequently considered "best quilts" in the South, where the winters are not severe enough to require heavy cover. We're very lucky to own many fine 1930s quilts, one of which is clearly a masterpiece: the *Orchid Wreath Appliqué* from Emporia, Kansas, whose sister quilt by designer Rose Kretsinger is featured on the cover of one of the most beloved books in the quilt world, *Romance of the Patchwork Quilt in America*. The *Orchid Wreath* is like a rich dessert—it has absolutely everything: artistic appliqué, an elaborate design, luscious colors,

Orchid Wreath Applique, for quilt details see page 56

Celebrate Great Quilts!

incredible quilting, cotton sateens that feel like whipped cream, a gracefully curved inner and outer border, and to top it off—a double-piped binding. No one could ask for more.

But we do. We're always asking for more! And we're always finding more. Who knows what the rest of the twentyfirst century will bring as we continue our collecting adventure? Even after more than a quarter century of collecting, and hundreds of quilts tucked safely away in their acid-free boxes, carefully padded with their acid-free tissue paper, stored in a climate-controlled area, we're still adding to our collection. We never tire of finding quilts, discovering their secrets, and sharing their beauty with other people through exhibits, not only those at the International Quilt Festival but also in museum exhibitions such as those seen at the New England Quilt Museum and the Museum of Fine Arts-Houston, among others.

We know there are collectors who prefer to keep their collections private, believing that displaying the quilts is hard on them. We can understand that concern. We know there are collectors who assemble spectacular collections and eventually dispose of them at auction for high prices. We think that's exciting because it reinforces the value of quilts in the public's mind. There are other collectors who specialize and develop collections that are very finely focused on a specific type of quilt. We admire their discipline, for when those collections are brought to light, we learn much more about that kind of quilt from its context within the collection than we could ever learn by seeing the quilts individually.

"But we collect with our hearts, not our heads."

And just as we love the quilts we collect, we love to share them with others in the hope that seeing these pieces will enhance people's appreciation for their own quilts and for those family heirlooms that may be hidden away in a closet, sometimes for generations. We want to increase people's knowledge of quilts by exhibiting them, pointing out what makes them special, and telling their stories. In sharing with part of this tradition, to take up quilting, and to help keep this rewarding art alive. We believe that quilts are made to be enjoyed, and collecting quilts has truly been a joy to us.

Karey Patterson Bresenhan and
Nancy O'Bryant Puentes

1825–1849

- ◆Proliferation of roller-printed fabrics used in quilts, with ombré stripes and overprinted motifs seen

- ◆Roller-printed pillar designs similar to earlier ones

- ◆Unusual background prints, such as honeycombs and trellises, produced by roller printing

- ◆Small-scale stylized designs such as coral, seaweed, dots, leaves, berries

- ◆Shades of browns, blue-greens, purples, and lavenders

- ◆Large polka dots

Broderie Perse | Circa 1835; Ohio | *75" x 75"; Cotton and chintz; Hand embroidered, hand appliquéd, and hand quilted using 11 stitches per inch.*

This early Broderie Perse quilt has English chintz cutouts, which are sewed onto a foundation; the quilt was then finely and heavily quilted. The appliqué stitching in this quilt is nearly invisible. There is a wide border of slightly different white fabric that frames the lavish swags of floral chintz.

Lone Star

Circa 1845

98" x 98"; Cotton and chintz; Hand pieced and hand quilted using 6 stitches per inch.

This Lone Star would be striking enough with the prints used to make it, but coupled with the chintz background fabric in a larger-scale floral, it pulsates.

Bars & Roses

Circa 1845; Ohio

87" x 92"; Cotton; Hand pieced, hand appliquéd, and hand quilted using 14 stitches per inch.

Fine, close hand quilting completes this perfect example of an appliquéd strippy quilt. Solid red and deep green bars alternate with appliquéd and reverse appliqué roses, vines and leaves. The late Sandra Mitchell originally collected this quilt, which is featured in an article about the legendary quilt dealer in *Quilt Digest 4*, published in 1986.

Calimanco Quilt | Circa 1825 | *84" x 85"; Wool; Hand embroidered, hand pieced, and hand quilted using 6 stitches per inch.*

Calimanco is a type of glazed wool popular with quilters in the early decades of the nineteenth century. A heating process "glazed" wool and that gave it an elegant, shiny surface, which quiltmakers embellished with elaborate designs. In this unusual example, embroidered floral designs enhance the brown calimanco. Flowers and stars are quilted throughout and there is a feathered medallion quilted into the center of the quilt. The brown of this quilt is an unusually rich shade, possibly hand-dyed.

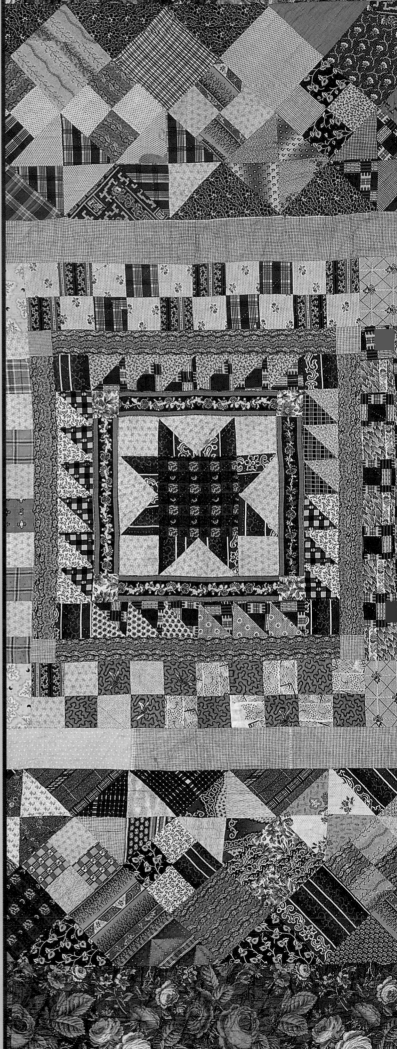

1850–1874

- ◆Invention of modern aniline dyes resulted in bright, crisp colors in fabrics

- ◆Prints based on woven textures such as moirés were common

- ◆Background shades of white with tiny geometric-shaped prints

- ◆"Conversation" prints with such popular motifs as horse heads, foxes, hammers, stirrups, dominoes, and insects appeared

- ◆Tiny flower prints outlined in black

- ◆Patriotic motifs commemorating the centennial, such as flags, eagles, and so on introduced

Rising Sun (or Sunburst)

Circa 1850, attributed to Cornelia Ann Schenck; Flatbush, New York

82" x 108": Cotton and chintz; Hand and machine pieced, hand quilted.

Radiating from the center of this quilt are diamonds in small floral and striped prints. It is bound with braid and the back of this quilt is glazed roller chintz with flowers and stripes in browns, creams, dark blues, and dark greens. In pristine condition, this quilt is unwashed and likely never used. It is a rarely seen pattern because it was so difficult to piece. An identical, possibly the same, quilt is pictured in the Orlofskys' *Quilts in America*. Abbeville Press, Inc.; Reprint edition (October 1992).

Flowers & Birds Appliqué

Circa 1850; Pennsylvania

88" x 90" (blocks are 15½" x 15½"; Cotton; Hand appliquéd, trapunto, and hand quilted using 8 stitches per inch.

It's unusual to find all the appliqué designs in a quilt also worked in trapunto, especially as heavily stuffed as they are in this one. A three-sided, wide swag border has clamshell quilting, and the center of the quilt is quilted on the diagonal. Each of the twenty birds in this design sports an embroidered eye.

Lone Star | Circa 1855 | *108" x 108"; Cotton; Hand pieced, hand appliquéd, and hand quilted using 8 stitches per inch.*

An unusual Lone Star variation, this has five smaller stars in each corner and one in the center of each side. In this version, there are sixteen points rather than the more traditional eight points on each star. The use of muslin diamonds to divide the darker colored bands makes this quilt seem to visually explode.

Celebrate Great Quilts!

Star Spangled Banner

Circa 1860

*84" x 86" (blocks measure 34" x 34");
Cotton; Hand pieced and hand quilted
using 10 stitches per inch.*

This quilt has four large Star Spangled Banner blocks surrounded by an unusual Basket of Flowers border, reminiscent of the fancy appliqué quilts popular at the time. It is intricately quilted in some areas. This Feathered Star pattern was the original logo of International Quilt Festival.

Center Medallion

Circa 1850

*92" x 84" (center block measures
11" x 11"); Cotton; Hand pieced and
hand quilted using 5 stitches per inch.*

This early Center Medallion has an 11" block with an eight-pointed Sawtooth Star at its heart. The rest of the quilt is constructed of a series of printed-cottons and glazed chintz borders, making it an unusual and complex quilt. The colors are particularly rich and appealing.

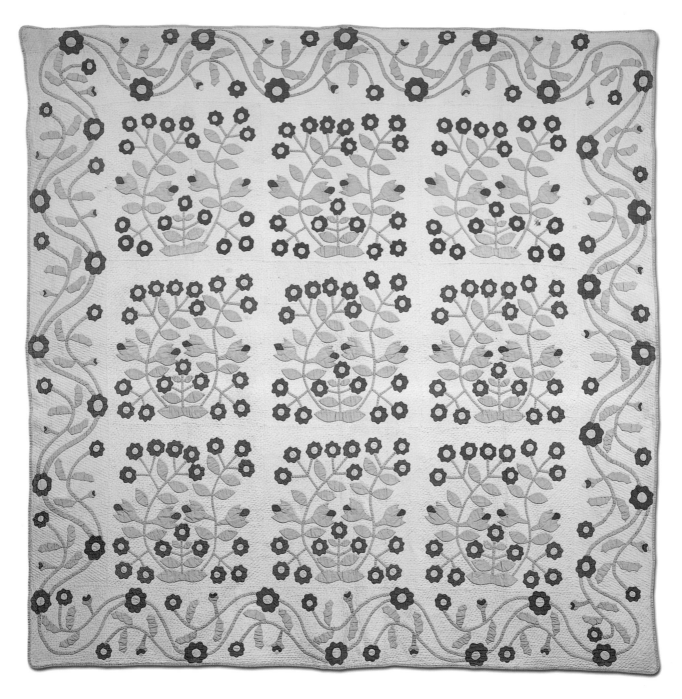

Oval Wreath with Flowers & Buds | **Circa 1860; from a southern state** | *84" x 84"; Cotton; Hand appliquéd and hand quilted using 13 stitches per inch.*

A most unusual, wide double-vine border encloses the central blocks in a classic open-wreath appliqué design, in red and green with yellow accents, on muslin. Beautifully quilted, with ¼" between the rows of stitches, the colors have faded gradually to the soft shades you see today.

Tulip (or Pomegranate) Stuffed Appliqué

Circa 1855

93¹/₂" x 94¹/₂" (blocks measure 13" x 13"); Cotton; hand appliquéd with piped borders.

Heavily hand stuffed, this quilt is finely appliquéd as well as quilted. The quilting is in quadruple crosshatch rows, with the border quilted in diagonal lines. The hand-applied binding has an inner double piping, one red and one green, followed by the applied binding edge in the same cream cotton as the rest of the quilt. The red used in the flowers is showing signs of wear, possibly from the heavy stuffing.

Flowers & Coxcombs

Circa 1860

90" x 90"; blocks measure 22¹/₂" x 22¹/₂"; Cotton; Hand pieced, hand appliquéd, and hand quilted using 6 stitches per inch.

The "pink" background for the appliqué in what looks like a rose-colored quilt is actually a fine red and white stripe. Appliqué, reverse appliqué, and double appliqué are all intricately done. The backing is strip pieced in bars of alternating red and yellow prints, making this quilt reversible.

Cherry Wreath │ Circa 1860 │ *82" x 83" (blocks measure 16" x 16"); Cotton; Hand appliquéd, and hand quilted using 13 stitches per inch.*

This classic *Cherry Wreath* is a formal design of sixteen elaborate wreaths centered by different floral motifs, all surrounded by a beautiful cherry-and-leaf vine border. Made in solid red and green with a few yellow accents, it is a perfect showcase for a master quiltmaker capable of exquisite workmanship.

Rose of Sharon variation | Circa 1860; Tennessee | *88" x 88" (blocks measure 30" x 30"); Cotton; Hand appliquéd and hand quilted using 8 stitches per inch.*

An early four-block Rose of Sharon variation in red, cheddar, green, and white featuring appliqué and reverse appliqué. It has an elaborate 13" border and feather quilting. Although it is in poor condition, the vivacious appeal of this quilt is undiminished.

Pots of Flowers with Stars | Circa 1865 | *76" x 84"; Cotton; Hand pieced, hand appliquéd, and hand quilted using 7 stitches per inch.*

Truly an original design, this intricately pieced and appliquéd nineteenth-century quilt has no customary name. Its complicated pieced and appliquéd motifs fill virtually every available space. It is a charming, idiosyncratic design with the verve and style that appealed to its original collector, the late Sandra Mitchell.

Celebrate Great Quilts!

President's Wreath

Circa 1865

*87" x 88" (blocks are 17½" x 17½");
Cotton; Hand appliquéd and hand
quilted using 8 stitches per inch.*

Present's Wreath is a design
dating back to the colonial
era. This example has nine blocks,
with white sashing and 6" corner
blocks. The wide appliqué border
features tulips and roses designed
to turn the corners perfectly.

Touching Stars

Circa 1865; Pennsylvania

*80" x 84" (blocks measure 26½" x 28");
Cotton; Hand and machine pieced, hand
appliquéd, and hand quilted using
7–8 stitches per inch.*

This dramatic Lone Star variation quilt consists of red,
green, and blue fabrics set on
muslin. The center of each large star
is of a tiny pink check, which is also
repeated in the rays of the stars. The
small red stars are hand pieced and
appliquéd; the large stars are also
hand pieced. Crosshatch quilting
completes the design. Karey loves
this quilt and often displays it on
her living room wall.

Moss Rose

Circa 1865, Josephine L_ _ _ han

77" x 84"; Cotton; Hand appliquéd and hand quilted.

Appliquéd Moss Rose blocks are set on point with partial blocks as joining triangles. With a gorgeous swag border with buds and tassels, the quilt is completed by red piping along the bound edge. It is signed Josephine L_ _ _ han (possibly Lanahan). Delicate embroidery forms the distinctive "mossy" parts of the rosebuds.

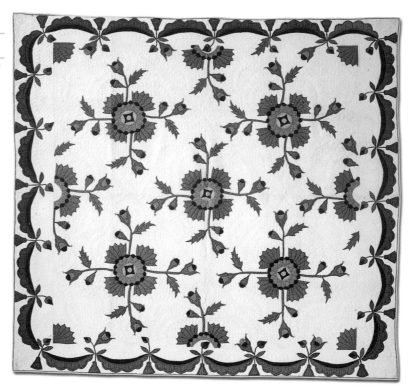

Rose of Sharon with Birds

Top circa 1865, appliquéd by an unknown quiltmaker in Connecticut; Hand quilted in 1993 by Valeta Edwards of Timpson, Texas.

85" x 104" (blocks measure 19" x 19"); Cotton and cotton sateen; Hand appliquéd and hand quilted using 9–10 stitches per inch.

Both the original appliqué and the 1993 quilting are exceptionally fine, even though the quilter noted that the thickness of the batting made it difficult to quilt. The charming, folky birds and flowers of the border offset the traditional, formal appliqué design in the Rose of Sharon blocks.

Contained Crazy or Album Quilt | Circa 1870; Pennsylvania | _70" x 79" (blocks measure 6½" x 6½"); Cotton; Hand pieced, hand appliquéd, hand quilted._

Made during the post Civil War era, this is an early, restrained and unadorned block-style Crazy Quilt, without the embroidery so typical of this genre. Its 72 unique blocks are contained within a lattice of red and black calico sashing with yellow calico stars at the junctures of the lattice, giving it a strong, unified look even though the composition is busy. Many of the blocks are recognizable quilt patterns—including the Flying Geese, Log Cabin, Basket, Chevron, Four Patch, Bear's Paw, and more—but we think the most charming block is the one with four hearts. This quilt was collected by Karey and her mother together, because alone, neither had enough money to buy it!

Baltimore Snowflakes

Circa 1865

101" x 102"; Cotton; Hand appliquéd and hand quilted using 10 stitches per inch.

A classic Baltimore Album block, these red snowflakes were created by folding and cutting in the German tradition of *scherenschnitte* ("scissor snips") or cut-paper appliqué. Green leaves were cut separately and probably appliquéd down prior to the snowflakes. The Victorian swag-and-bow border turns the corners beautifully at the bottom of the quilt and is anchored there by a red bow. The top of the quilt has four swags while the other sides have five.

Note the graceful tails of the bows and the double stair-step borders.

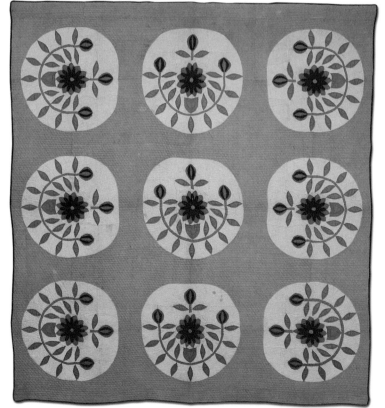

Prairie Flower

Circa 1870

78" x 83", 21" circle; Cotton; Hand pieced and hand quilted using approximately 9 stitches per inch.

Traditionally an appliqué pattern, this quilt design is almost entirely pieced instead, a feat hard to imagine, especially because appliquéd Prairie Flower quilts were popular at the time and would have been much less difficult to make.

Birds & Grapes Appliqué | Circa 1870 | *77" x 82" (blocks are 24" x 24"); Cotton; Hand appliquéd and hand quilted using 9 stitches per inch.*

The four large Princess Feather blocks that form the center of this elaborate quilt are just the beginning of its complex motifs. Flowers radiate from the center of the blocks between the "feathers" and are also placed in the center of the design. A 14½" border features birds with embroidered eyes, poised to eat grapes growing on a sinuous vine.

Garden Maze with Shoo Fly

Circa 1870; New England

76" x 88" (blocks measure 15" x 15"); Cotton; Hand pieced and hand quilted using 6 stitches per inch.

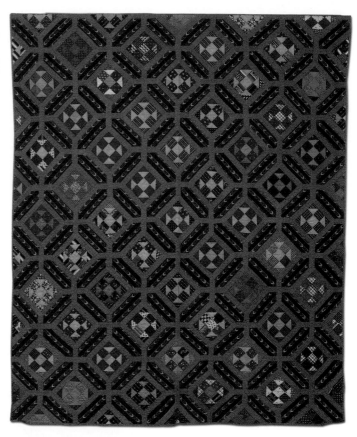

This is a richly colored quilt featuring Garden Maze blocks set on point, with Shoo Fly blocks forming the centers. The diagonal set, Garden Maze sashing, and intense colors make this a knockout quilt. Many of the rich copper colored prints typical of this period are seen in this quilt.

Sunburst

Circa 1870; Central Texas

74½" x 80½" (blocks measure 37" x 37"); Cotton (possibly linen); Hand pieced and hand quilted using 6 stitches per inch.

Another large, bold, four-block design, this quilt was made in red and gold, and hand pieced and quilted in the difficult Sunburst pattern. The small, red square in the center of the gold sashing and the feather design quilted into the block corners and two borders are special touches. The backing fabric appears to be homespun.

Log Cabin: Chimneys & Cornerstones variation | Circa 1870 | *68¹/₂" x 81"; Cotton with wool center squares; Hand pieced and hand quilted.*

Tiny logs, measuring ¹/₄" when finished and made in calico prints, solids, plaids, checks, and stripes, were used for these blocks, centered with red wool. The 3" Log Cabin blocks create the distinct grid pattern through the placement of light and dark fabrics. It was typical of such a quilt to be finished with only a simple binding, no borders. Its solid red backing is a nice surprise.

1875–1899

♦Larger motifs such as bells, riding crops and horseshoes, anchors, and the like used in shirting fabrics found their way into quilts

♦Increased popularity of roller prints

♦Further use of commemorative fabrics in quilts

♦Designs appearing in several colorways grew in popularity

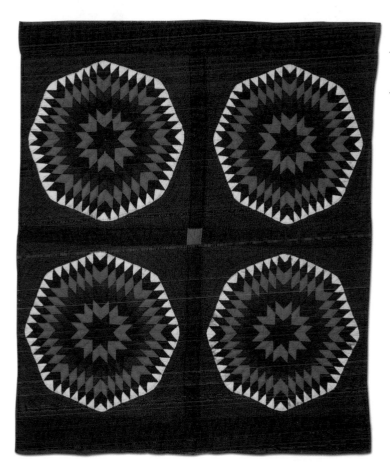

Blazing Star

Circa 1875, Mary Denman; Lufkin, Texas

69" x 82" (blocks measure 32" x 32"); Cotton; Hand pieced using 3–4 stitches per inch.

Dynamic design makes up for casual workmanship in this classic Texas country quilt. Vivid colors and a simple four-block design are offset by thick cotton batting and big stitches to produce a visually arresting quilt. The pattern is also known as Sunburst.

Pine Tree
—
Circa 1880

71½" x 92" (blocks measure 17½" x 17½"); Cotton; Hand pieced and hand quilted using 7 stitches per inch.

The traditional Pine Tree block, is also known as the Tree of Life block. Red and green calicoes on a muslin background make this an appealing quilt to use during the holidays.

Snowflake | Circa 1880, Unknown Mennonite; Lancaster County, Pennsylvania | *84 ¹/₂" x 84¹/₂" (blocks measure 18" x 18"); Cotton; Hand pieced, hand appliquéd, and hand quilted.*

This Mennonite quilt is beautiful to display during the holiday season with its green and red Snowflake design with gold flowers with red centers, a red diamond inner border, and wide, green outer border. Mennonite quilters liked rich colors and often set their deeply saturated appliqués on non-contrasting backgrounds.

Princess Feather

Circa 1880; Pennsylvania

*84¹/2" x 86" (blocks measure 31" x 31");
Cotton; Hand appliquéd and hand
quilted using 11 stitches per inch.*

In perfect condition, this four-block Princess Feather variation with stars has a wonderful swag border that turns the corners perfectly. Its dark greens, reds, and cheddars are set off on a white background with exquisite quilting. Originally collected by the late Sandra Mitchell, a frequent exhibitor at International Quilt Festival.

Carpenter's Square

Circa 1880

*7,3" x 74" (blocks average 23¹/2" x 23¹/2");
Cotton; Pieced and quilted by hand and
machine.*

An indigo and white Carpenter's Square is distinguished by an unusual diagonal block. Constructed by hand and machine, the quilt features double-line hand quilting in a windowpane pattern with a hand-stitched binding.

Log Cabin: Pineapple or Windmill Blades variation | Circa 1880 | *78¹/₂" x 84¹/₂" (blocks measure 12" x 12"); Cotton; Hand pieced and machine quilted using 9 stitches per inch.*

The 4" zigzag border of black-and-white shirting fabric on green calico sets off this optical, pulsating Log Cabin in the Pineapple variation. The extraordinary backing fabric is red and brown calico flowers, fruit, and birds.

Star of Bethlehem | Circa 1880, Unknown Mennonite; Pennsylvania | *80" x 80"; Cotton; Pieced and hand quilted using 7 stitches per inch.*

A striking Star of Bethlehem, or Lone Star, this pieced quilt has stars and half-stars appliquéd on the setting. Cable wreaths are quilted in the corners with an inner feather wreath, and feathers and baskets are quilted in the border. The vibrant colors enhance the simplicity of this dramatic design.

Nine-Patch Checkerboard

Circa 1885

—

66" x 69"; Cotton; Hand pieced and hand quilted using 7 stitches per inch.

This pattern was also called Grandmother's Pride, Old Mail, the Queen's Favorite, and Checkerboard when slightly different placements of the light and medium fabrics were used. The quilter's use of two Sawtooth borders is unusual.

Log Cabin: Barn Raising variation

Circa 1880

—

83" x 75" (blocks are 8½" x 8½"); Cotton; Hand pieced and hand quilted.

The most interesting thing about this handsome Log Cabin in the Barn Raising variation is that it isn't square. This moves the central design off center. The back of this quilt is wool paisley.

Crazy Quilt | Circa **1885** | *56½" x 57½"; Silks and velvets; Hand embroidered and hand painted.*

A magnificent schooner flying the American flag forms the Medallion center of this Crazy Quilt of silks and velvets encrusted with intricate embroidery stitches. Motifs abound in this elaborately embroidered and hand-painted quilt. The famous schooner "America"—which the America's Cup was named for when it broke Britain's hold on yacht racing championships in 1851—may have been the inspiration for the center block. It closely resembles depictions of the original "America," even down to the placement of the flag.

Carpenter's Square

—

Circa 1895

—

73" x 73"; Cotton; Hand pieced and hand quilted using 9 stitches per inch.

This red and white modified *Carpenter's Square* is combined and repeated with interlaced blocks to form the top. The two slightly different blocks and the sashing are joined in such a way that five interlocking and overlapping larger blocks are formed. The hand quilting is impeccable.

President's Medallion

—

Circa 1889—dated in center block, Pennsylvania

80¹⁄₂" x 81" (squares 2¹⁄₂"; blocks are 7¹⁄₂" x 7¹⁄₂"); Cotton, commemorative handkerchief, backed with Columbia Star "cheater" cloth; Hand pieced and hand quilted using 7 stitches per inch.

A handkerchief with portraits of presidents George Washington and Benjamin Harrison—produced to mark 100 years of the American presidency from 1789 to 1889—serves as the center medallion of this quilt. The handkerchief is surrounded by small pieced squares of conversation prints arranged to form a series of dramatic diamond shapes framing and emphasizing the central motif. Conversation prints are tiny, detailed prints of realistic insects, animals, faces, fire engines, whips, spurs, and the like.

Wild Goose Chase variation with Floral Border | Circa 1890; Signed in center in the quilting Amanda M. Reichars, Texas | *76" x 93" (blocks measure 18" x 18"); Cotton, pieced, hand appliquéd, and hand quilted using 8 stitches per inch.*

This complex design mystifies even experienced quiltmakers as they puzzle over its construction. The impact of this two-color quilt with its two Sawtooth borders and unique appliquéd floral border is intriguing.

Log Cabin: Courthouse Steps variation | Circa 1890 | *65" x 65" (block 4" x 4"); Silk; Hand pieced and hand quilted, with a machine-sewn binding.*

Courthouse Steps is the Log Cabin variation used in this quilt. It's made of solid color silk "logs" arranged so that the 4" blocks create larger 8" blocks. Repetition of the design motif creates a dramatic quilt, emphasized by the lush fabrics.

Pineapple Appliqué | Top circa 1890, appliquéd and pieced; Machine quilted in 2003 by Kathy Colvin, Richmond, Texas | *85" x 104"; Cotton; Hand pieced and hand appliquéd, then machine quilted in 2003.*

This Pineapple was appliquéd and pieced by hand between 1885–1895, and machine quilted in 2003. At that time two small borders of cheddar and muslin were added and the quilt was bound with cheddar. Vicki Mangum, manager of Festival's special exhibits dyed the newly added cheddar to match the original. The Pineapple pattern was often used to convey hospitality; this is an unusual design that uses tiny triangles to depict the surface of the fruit.

Thistles & Currants

Circa 1885

75½" x 75½" (blocks are 10½" by 10½");
Cotton; Hand appliquéd and hand quilted
using 8 stitches per inch.

Once dark green, many portions of this beautifully appliquéd quilt have faded to gray, an example of what is called a "fugitive," or unstable, dye. A wonderful old pattern that is seldom seen, this quilt has a thistle border that turns all but one corner.

Rose of Sharon with Pomegranates

Circa 1890

81" x 101" (blocks measure 33" x 28 ½");
Cotton; Hand appliquéd and hand quilted
using 11 stitches per inch.

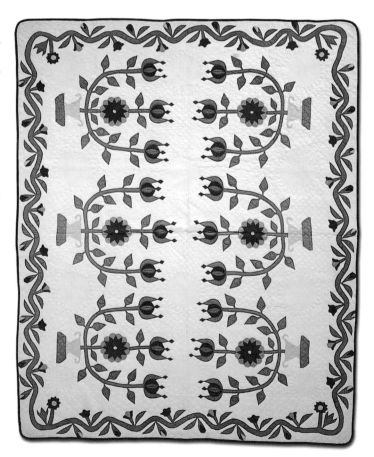

Beautiful quilting and a fancy 7½" appliquéd flower-and-bud vine border make this Rose of Sharon variation unique. The border design turns all four corners neatly. Without its pots, this design has a clear kinship to the Prairie Flower (page 26).

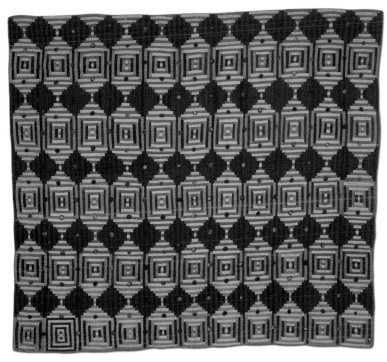

Log Cabin: Courthouse Steps variation

Circa 1890

80½" x 74" (blocks are 6" x 6"); Possibly homespun and silk, with cotton twill for piecework; Foundation pieced, hand quilted using 7 stitches per inch, and hand tied.

This Courthouse Steps variation features blocks foundation pieced onto coarse muslin, feed sacking, or homespun. Silk and cotton twill is used in the piecework. It is both hand quilted and hand tied with variegated wool yarn, which forms rosettes in the center of each block. The backing is polished cotton in a surprising black and red rose print.

Lone Star

Top circa 1875. Machine quilted in 2003 by Kathy Colvin of Richmond, Texas.

96" x 98"; Cotton; Hand pieced, then machine quilted in 2003.

This unusual seven-pointed Lone Star was hand pieced in the nineteenth century and long-arm machine quilted in the twenty-first. Sixteen cotton fabrics are featured, including one polished cotton. Its intricate feather quilting was specifically designed to fill each of the background spaces with ribbon or scroll work.

Log Cabin: Barn Raising variation

—

Circa 1890

—

*73¼" x 72¼" (blocks are 10" x 10");
Silk; Hand foundation pieced and hand
quilted using 5 stitches per inch.*

This silk Victorian Log Cabin was hand pieced onto a fabric foundation, then hand quilted. There are strip-pieced borders and one plaid border adding to the handsome, overall graphic effect.

Nine-Patch Criss-Cross

Circa 1895, Unknown Mennonite;
Canada

*71½" x 83" (blocks measure 10", sashing
measures 1½"); Wool; Hand pieced and hand
quilted using 9 stitches per inch.*

Wool in predominantly blues, pinks, and greens are employed for a dramatic effect in this hand pieced and quilted quilt made by a master quilter who wanted to create something a little different. She used a combination of two blocks called, variously, Pennsylvania, Simple Cross, Single Irish Chain, Criss-Cross, Alabama, Squares and Oblongs, or Geometric Block.

Holly & Berries | Circa 1890 | *82" x 86" (blocks are 23" x 22"); Cotton; Hand appliquéd and hand quilted.*

Nine blocks have solid dark blue-green holly and solid red berries. A Sawtooth border and sashing, and a spindly berry design set off the blocks, and the vines in the 8" border. The design is delightful but does not turn the corners.

Tree of Life variation
—
Circa 1895

*72" x 76" (blocks measure 19" x 19");
Cotton; Machine pieced, hand appliquéd,
and hand quilted using 7 stitches
per inch.*

With nine blocks featuring a dozen free-form flowers in blue pots, this deceptively naïve quilt is probably an original design. It is hand appliquéd and hand quilted; blocks are sewn together by machine. A charming folk-art quilt!

Pine Tree
—
Circa 1895, possibly Mennonite; Pennsylvania
—
*89" x 89" (blocks are 18½" x 18½");
Cotton; Machine pieced and hand
quilted using 9 stitches per inch.*

This is a traditional red and green Pine Tree, or Tree of Life, thought to be made by a Mennonite quilter. Red, olive drab, and khaki cotton are used on the top, while the back combines rust and indigo prints in a Bars design that makes the quilt reversible.

Scherenschnitte Quilt | Circa 1895 | *75" x 77" (blocks measure 21" x 21"); Cotton; Hand appliquéd and hand quilted using 7 stitches per inch.*

Scherenschnitte, or cut-paper appliqué, is the technique used in this beautiful red and white Snowflake quilt. Thirteen different Snowflake designs make a wonderful winter quilt.

1900–1924

◆ Much Art Deco influenced design
appears in prints

◆ Pastels proliferated in roller-printed
fabrics

◆ Calicoes of an earlier period contin-
ued, but prints are larger scale and
less intricate

◆ White background shades with
much brighter prints found

Sunshine & Shadow

Circa 1900, Esther Weber; Reading, Pennsylvania

83" x 81"; Cotton; Hand pieced and hand quilted using 9 stitches per inch. Unlined.

The center in this Mennonite quilt appears to be older than its gray and red borders with their cable patterned quilting design. The family name for this Trip Around the World variation was Bowmansville Star.

Lone Star

Circa 1900

85½" x 88"; Cotton, Hand pieced and hand quilted using 6 stitches per inch.

A vividly hued Lone Star with blue print inserts at corners and between the points of the star, it is quilted with only six stitches to the inch. This was not uncommon, as the piecing, rather than quilting, is what the quilter was usually showing off. The Sawtooth border contains this star nicely.

Feathered Stars & Redwork | Circa 1900; Ohio | *88" x 90" (center medallion 25¹⁄₃" x 25¹⁄₂"); Cotton; Hand pieced, hand embroidered, and hand quilted using 9 stitches per inch.*

Elaborate Feathered Stars are pieced in red on white, and fancy redwork flowers and leaves—each of a different design—fill the white background of this gorgeous quilt. A large central Medallion block contains an embroidered, feathered wreath surrounding a redwork snowflake with a crosshatch center. There is a Sawtooth outside border, a quilted white inner border, and another inner Sawtooth border. This quilt was acquired from the Sandra Mitchell estate.

Modified Nine-Patch

Circa 1920, Unknown Amish Quilter; Holmes County, Ohio

74" x 74" (blocks are 7 11/16" x 7 11/16"); Cotton and cotton sateens; Machine pieced and hand quilted using 8 stitches per inch.

This Nine Patch employs precise use of color and intensity within each block. The blocks were then rotated to create the impression of a Log Cabin (Barn Raising variation) with a secondary overlaid latticed design.

Log Cabin with Ohio Stars

Circa 1900

62½" x 62¾" (blocks are 14" x 14"); Cotton; Hand pieced and hand quilted using 6 stitches per inch.

Nine Log Cabin blocks set on point have tiny Ohio Star centers, and there are three 1" borders using blue, red, and yellow, with red binding in this hand pieced and hand quilted design. A quilted, feathered wreath centers the four muslin blocks. This is an especially charming, lively quilt.

String-Pieced Star
—
Circa 1920, Leana Powel Ada; Texas

72" x 80"; Cotton; Hand pieced and hand quilted using 9 stitches per inch.

This controlled Strip- or String-Pieced Star has all the impact of a Lone Star. Light background shirting fabric sets off the calicoes and solids used in the star, and a wide border on the bottom lengthens the quilt.

Floral Embroidered Quilt
—
Circa 1900; Georgetown, Kentucky

89" x 89" (blocks average 17" x 17"); Wool; Hand pieced and embroidered with embroidery threads. Unlined and unquilted.

Multicolored floral designs are embroidered on black and white wool backgrounds. Briar stitching is used on all seams, and blocks are of various sizes with additional embroidered pieces used as needed to fill out the large squares. Simply bound, the quilt has no backing. This piece is a treasure of exuberant embroidery with all the bouquets facing the center.

1925–1940

◆ Flowered percales were used exten-
sively in quilts

◆ Novelty prints featuring such motifs
as children, rabbits, and the like
became extremely popular

String-Pieced Star
—
Circa 1930, Bobbie Dale Kerns; Camden, Indiana
—
80" x 86"; Cotton; Machine pieced and hand quilted.

Start with an uncommon five-pointed String-Pieced Star, surround it with ten smaller ones forming a circle. Then add four borders—two solid white and two pieced out of colorful fabrics—and then quilt feathers between the big star and its encircling smaller stars. What you end up with is a quilt that might well have been this quiltmaker's original design. A delight for anyone who collects five-pointed stars, as we do.

Ocean Wave with Stars
—
Circa 1925, Unknown Amish; Holmes County, Ohio
—
74" x 75" (blocks are 9" x 9"); Cotton; Machine pieced and hand quilted using 9 stitches per inch;

Solid cotton sateen is machine pieced in two patterns and hand quilted. It's somewhat unusual for an Amish quilter to combine patterns, but Midwestern Amish quilts generally have more pieces and more colors than the severely geometric Amish quilts of Lancaster County, Pennsylvania.

Bear's Paw | Circa 1925, Unknown Amish; Holmes County, Ohio | *73" x 76" (blocks are 15" x 15"); Cotton, cotton sateen, twill (wool possibly); Machine pieced and hand quilted using 9 stitches per inch.*

This Midwestern Amish quilt is blue and black, featuring cable quilting. Nine Bear's Paw blocks have a 6" sashing, an inner blue border, and a wide black outer border. Amish quilters often use fabrics close in color value while most other quilters prefer contrasting colors.

Orchid Wreath Appliqué

Circa 1930, designed by Rose Kretsinger, maker
unknown; Emporia, Kansas

—

*89" x 89"; Cotton; Hand appliquéd and hand quilted using
9 stitches per inch.*

In quilter's nomenclature of the day, a quilt made "on the halves" meant that when a quilter made a quilt to be featured in a book, that quilter would receive the fabric and the rights to make another "sister quilt" to keep for herself.

This historic quilt is thought to be the sister quilt of the quilt featured on the cover of the book *The Romance of Patchwork Quilts in America* by Carrie A. Hall and Rose Kretsinger (Outlet, 1988).

This gorgeous tour de force has superb appliqué, piecing, reverse appliqué, and hand quilting, contains all cotton sateen fabrics, and its border, a Kretsinger design, is finished with a double corded binding. The original Rose Kretsinger design was named as one of the The 20th Century's 100 Best American Quilts.

Horn of Plenty

—

Circa 1930; Missouri

—

*83" x 88" (blocks are 16 1/2" x 18");
Cotton sateens; Hand appliquéd and hand
quilted.*

This fine example of 1930s hand appliqué is also known as Cornucopia, and features eight baskets of flowers around a center block filled with flowers. It's made with solid-color cotton sateens, has an elaborate floral appliqué inner border, a scalloped aqua outer border that echoes the aqua sashing, and is finished with a bound border. It is beautifully hand quilted.

Celebrate Great Quilts!

Broken Star | Circa 1930, Myrtle Augusta Loomis Patterson; Gilmer, Texas | *84" x 84" (blocks measure 11" x 11"); Cotton; Hand pieced and hand quilted using 8 stitches per inch.*

Using a kit with solid-color cottons and two borders—one red, one muslin—this beautiful Broken Star was made by Karey's paternal grandmother, Myrtle Augusta Loomis Patterson. It was part of Karey's father's "hope chest" of eight quilts, made by a woman who sent both her sons into marriage with their own "dowry" of quilts. It features red and muslin four patches in each corner. Mrs. Patterson made a Lone Star quilt from a matching kit, and had it quilted by the Works Progress Administration (WPA). This one, a more complex Broken Star, she quilted herself.

Vase of Tulips

Circa 1930; Midwest

81" x 105" (blocks are 15½" x 15½"); Cotton; Machine pieced blocks, hand appliquéd, and hand quilted using 9 stitches per inch.

Made from a mail-order pattern or a kit, this attractive quilt features twelve bouquets of pink, orchid, and yellow tulips in blue vases on a white background. A sunflower design is quilted in the blocks between the appliquéd blocks, and the pretty scalloped-edge border has appliquéd tulips.

Basket of Flowers

Circa 1930, Appliquéd; 1992, quilted by unknown.

88" x 88" (blocks measure 15½" x 15½"); Cotton; Hand and machine pieced, hand appliquéd, and hand quilted using 6–7 stitches per inch.

A 30's appliqué with a 5½" ice cream cone border, this is an unusual quilt. Yo-yos are used for flowers in blocks set on point with two-inch sashing that forms a grid.

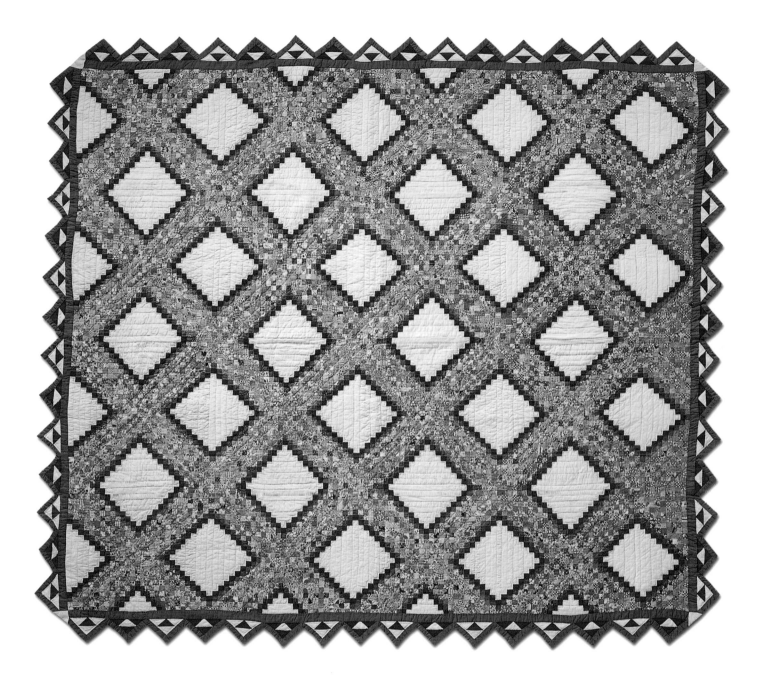

Postage Stamp | Circa 1930; Illinois | *88" x 76"; Cotton; Pieced and hand quilted using 7 stitches per inch.*

This great Irish Chain variation has solids, prints, and calicoes in the postage-stamp sized pieces. What makes it so unique, however, is the unusual, and highly elaborate, Sawtooth pieced border.

Sunshine & Shadow | Circa 1935 | *82" x 82"; Cotton, wool; Machine pieced and hand quilted using 9 stitches per inch.*

A variation of Trip Around the World, this Sunshine and Shadow is made of cotton and wool. This is a good example of how the use of borders can give a quilt extra drama. A flower motif is quilted into the wide, black border, while the green border has modified cable quilting.

Lover's Knot | Circa 1940 Myrtle Augusta Loomis Patterson, Gilmer, Texas | *85" x 88"; blocks measure 10½" x 11"; Cotton; Hand pieced and hand quilted. Each piece is double-quilted around both sides of the design through cotton batting.*

Each block of this old-fashioned scrap quilt has a print fabric and a solid, set on a muslin back ground. This design offers an attractive way to use up an extensive collection of scrap fabrics, not often seen in quilts today. Karey's paternal grandmother, who loved to piece but not to quilt, made this. She used quilters from the Works Progress Administration (WPA), who quilted for 10¢ per spool of thread used.

INDEX

ABOUT the AUTHORS

Karey is the president of Quilts, Inc. and director of the International Quilt Markets and International Quilt Festivals. Karey's business acumen, enthusiasm for quilting, and perseverance helped her create and foster the quilting industry, now worth $2.27 billion a year in the U.S. and involving 21.3 American quilters.

An acknowledged expert on quilt dating, Karey was named to the Quilters Hall of Fame and is the author or co-author of five quilt reference books and guest curator of museum exhibitions.

Nancy is executive vice-president of Quilts, Inc.; a co-founder of the International Quilt Association and editorial director of its journal, *Quilts: A World of Beauty*; and the author of numerous articles on quilts and quilting for consumer and industry publications.

Drawing on her interest in quilt conservation, Nancy coordinated a hands-on quilt conservation and restoration seminar and laboratory in 1984, the first to bring quilters, conservators, and museum professionals together. She also wrote the first book to address quilt care for the layman: *First Aid for Family Quilts*.

In addition to Karey and Nancy's co-founding the International Quilt Association (with their mothers) and The Alliance for American Quilts, the two 5th-generation Texas quilters have been a driving force in the growth of quilting in Europe, where they are co-directors of Patchwork & Quilt Expo—the major international quilt show held in Europe since 1988. As co-directors of the seven-year Texas Quilt Search and co-curators for the related museum exhibitions, together they co-authored the project's two award winning books: *Lone Stars: A legacy of Texas Quilts, Volumes I and II*.

Four of the Best Loved Quilt Patterns
from the *Celebrate Great Quilts!* Collection

$8.95 each

Modified Nine-Patch Pattern
76" x 76"

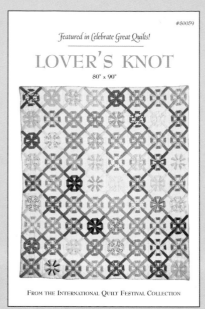

Lover's Knot Pattern
80" x 90"

Touching Stars Pattern
76.5" x 76.5"

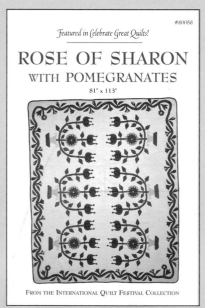

**Rose of Sharon with
Pomegranates Pattern**
81" x 113"

Place your order today at 800-284-1114 or www.ctpub.com